NORTHAMPTONSHIRE

Edited By Debbie Killingworth

First published in Great Britain in 2018 by:

 Young**Writers**

Young Writers
Remus House
Coltsfoot Drive
Peterborough
PE2 9BF
Telephone: 01733 890066
Website: www.youngwriters.co.uk

FOREWORD

Young Writers was created in 1991 with the express purpose of promoting and encouraging creative writing. Each competition we create is tailored to the relevant age group, hopefully giving each child the inspiration and incentive to create their own piece of writing, whether it's a poem or a short story. We truly believe that seeing it in print gives pupils a sense of achievement and pride in their work and themselves.

Our latest competition, Monster Poetry, focuses on uncovering the different techniques used in poetry and encouraging pupils to explore new ways to write a poem. Using a mix of imagination, expression and poetic styles, this anthology is an impressive snapshot of the inventive, original and skilful writing of young people today. These poems showcase the creativity and talent of these budding new writers as they learn the skills of writing, and we hope you are as entertained by them as we are.

CONTENTS

Amelia Woodcock (9) 64
Noah Sturges (7) 65
Sophie Ireson-Vaughan (9) 66
William Cruttwell (9) 67
Catherine Ward (8) 68
Brianna Starsmore (8) 69
Jude Ennis Drury (7) 70
Joel Smith (8) 71
Holly Greasley (9) 72
Callum Brooks (8) 73
Abi Daly (8) 74
Elliot Nicholls (9) 75
Lucy Terry (8) 76
Scarlett Breakell (7) 77
Lily Sales (8) 78
Skye Weatherley (8) 79
Neriah Angela Goodream-Wilson (8) 80

Irthlingborough Junior School, Irthlingborough

Levi Nelson (8) 81
Freddie Nicklin (11) & Zak Swinton 82
Saoirse Gibbard (9) 83
Oliver Andrews (10) & Thomas Ritchings 84
Keira Thomas (8) 85
Miley Louise Jackson (9) 86
Lana Eldridge (9) 87
Becky Bushby (9) 88
Katie Boardman (10) 89
Alexander Barley (8) 90
Natalie Robinson (9) 91

Overstone Park School, Northampton

Kai Ethan Filbee (8) 92
Jaylen Aaron Isaac Ferdinand (10) 93
Lauryn Morgan (9) 94

Stimpson Avenue Academy, Northampton

Patricia Alfaro Pereira (8) 95
Ummur Ali (8) 96
Faith Bainger (8) 98
Fayez Ahmed (8) 100
James Lawford Braithwaite (7) 101
Samuel Dwelly (9) 102
Zakk Carpenter (8) 103
Lola Akanmu (8) 104
Emma McFadian (8) 105
Areeba Islam (8) 106
Emilija Balceraite (9) 107
Sandra Baltag (8) 108
Shun Nyame (7) 109
Fin Shields (8) 110
Wiktoriq Seredynska (7) 111
Aida Vladi (8) 112
Raihana Kabeer (8) 113
Waseeur Rahman (8) 114
Mateusz Buczko (8) 115
Melchizedek N Poku (8) 116
Armands Mundiciems (8) 117
Ineta Alicia Ivanova (8) 118
Jake O'Connell (8) 119
Alex Plyoplev (8) 120
Zayna Ali (8) 121

The Spires Academy, Great Billing

Lillie Gallucci (10) 122
Allan Holland (11) 124
Alfie Green (10) 125
Kayleigh Holmes (10) 126
Finleigh Clewley (9) 127
Skye Louise Carter (11) 128
Logan Pegg (11) 129
Freddie Mayes (10) 130
Haylan Blomguist (8) 131
Jack Newton (10) 132

Walgrave Primary School, Walgrave

Bella Hooper (10)	133
Esther Hobbs (9)	134
Brannon Bird (10)	136
Thea Simons (9)	138
Wilson Sydney Wright (9)	140
Isla Charlotte McRae (10)	142
Isabelle Madeleine Murphy (9)	144
Olivia Sweeney (9)	146
Tom Benn (10)	148
Serena Megan Day (9)	150
Olivia Clarke (10)	152
Erin Lucie Day (9)	154
Chanel Fury (10)	156
Oliver Jeffery (9) & Harrison Singh Hammond	157
Iris Jones (9)	158
Shana Simone Odell (10)	159
Theo Collins (9)	160
Ed Bond (10)	161
Freya Elizabeth Perkins (10)	162
Poppie Davidson Murphy (9)	163
Isaac Ellis (9)	164
Tommy Hooper (9)	165
Joshua Sweet (10)	166
Fraser MacPhail (10)	167
Jessica-Louise Jeffery (10)	168
William Wren (9)	169
Charles William Howard Burditt (10)	170
Charlotte Murphy (10)	171
Taylor Linnell (10)	172
Darcie Quigley (9)	173
Kye Hansen (9)	174
Rachel Leonard (9)	175
Oscar Newberry (9)	176

THE POEMS

Lenny

Lenny was born in the Highlands
A monster colossal and fat
He is kind but he's scary
And people are wary
He'd even frighten your cat.

Don't worry, he's not at all lonely
He lives with his friend in a bog
And when people knock
They get a shock
Because Benny, his friend, is a dog.

One day his friend got unlucky
When he went to the shops on his own
He stood on a log
In a very deep bog
And said, "This is going to get mucky."

Now Lenny was just on his way
To go to the Bay of Biscay
He heard Benny yelp
And thought, *I better go help*
And saved his friend, Benny, hooray!

Samuel Alexander Martin (9)
Bracken Leas Primary School, Brackley

The Ugliest Creature

The ugliest creature
In the known universe
Is the pus-boiled Blobite.
For there's really nothing worse
Than his slimy, green scales
That had started to rot
And produce a foul smell
To make you vomit on the spot.

With one large cyclops eye
In the centre of his head
And six more on antennae
All crossed and bloodshot red.
He doesn't have a nose
But has two large yellow fangs
From which gloopy, yellow snot
Often drips or hangs.

I finally tracked him down
On his native planet Bong
Though he was very hard to look at
I could tell something was wrong.

Imagine my surprise
As he pointed three arms at me
And yelled, "Yuck, that Earth girl's
The ugliest creature I ever did see!"

Amelie Harford (8)

Bracken Leas Primary School, Brackley

Forever Friends

I heard a padding one night,
In he came, as quiet as a mouse.
2cm tall, 3cm wide,
In through the window, he invaded my house.

I woke up from bed,
Opened my eyes, got a bit of a fright.
There he was, on the end of my nose,
I reached for the switch and turned on the light.

He squeaked, "Where's the volcano?
I have a ritual tonight!"
"Why don't you stay, be my best friend?"
"Why not," he said, "it's comfy alright!"

And he is still with me now,
Munching his favourite food (dog treats).

Forever friends for evermore,
I still dream of the padding of our first meet.

Samuel Sellick (9)
Bracken Leas Primary School, Brackley

Binky Bob

Binky Bob lived on Planet Blirth
He bump, bump, bump, bumped down
He saw some big, big bullies on Earth
They really made him frown.

His wings spread out like a golden eagle
His horns popped out from the top of his head
His body wobbled like jelly beans
And his eyes were glowing fiery red.

The bullies turned slowly round
And jumped with horror and fright
Binky Bob roared like an earthquake
And they fled into the night.

Everybody cheered and everybody screamed
Binky Bob was the hero of the Earth
He got carried away helping out
And never went back to Planet Blirth.

Libby Porter (9)
Bracken Leas Primary School, Brackley

My Friendly Monster, Bubblegum

My friendly monster is called Bubblegum,
He's kind and furry and he's my best chum.
He wakes me up in the middle of the night,
So we have a pillow fight.
He's my favourite colour, a nice bright blue,
You won't find him at London Zoo
Because he comes from Ice Cream World,
He always looks smart and his hair is curled.
His friends are called Minty and Berry,
His favourite flavours are toffee and cherry.
He likes having bubblegum parties,
His favourite toppings are sprinkles and Smarties.
He likes running around the park twice
And he is very nice.

Katie Messer (9)
Bracken Leas Primary School, Brackley

Budy

Budy was a peculiar monster,
He was sad, fluffy and grumpy,
He had round hands and dirty teeth
That were the size of a bulldozer.
He had spiked-up hair.

He lived in England in Northamptonshire,
He liked watching TV with me
And played football with me a lot.
Budy enjoyed pretty much anything except Friends.
In fact his only friend was me,
He liked me because I took him everywhere.

We would go to the park and play football,
Budy was bad though,
When he kicked the ball
It always hit someone
Like a baby or a granny and he would laugh.

Max Samuel Goodman (9)
Bracken Leas Primary School, Brackley

Blobber

Meet Blobber, a slimy, five-eyed kinda guy.
He doesn't have any friends because he is quite shy.
With skin as green as grass and fangs as sharp as knives,
his hidden superpower comes from scoffing pies!
This quiet, slobbery fella hails from Loud Mouth Land
which explains why our gentle monster was rejected by the gang.
He discovered late one evening when he felt a hunger pang,
munching on a steak and kidney made him disappear with a bang.
This skill made him popular again, our super-powered Blobber
just because he's quiet, doesn't mean he has nothing to offer.

Nia Tynan (8)
Bracken Leas Primary School, Brackley

My Friend Carl

I have a monster friend named Carl,
Who came from a planet called Dejarl,
He now lives in a castle on a cloud
Where no one can hear him out loud.
He has five eyes and no nose,
He is a professional footballer but nobody knows.
He has wings so he can fly,
He does acrobatics in the sky,
He is very small and hairy
But not at all scary.
He has a long tongue to catch a frog,
His favourite friend is a bulldog.
My monster, Carl, is very clever
And the shoes he wears are made from leather.
If you ever need him here
Shout his name and he will appear!

Zac White (9)
Bracken Leas Primary School, Brackley

What Monsters Are Like!

This is what monsters do,
This is what monsters do,
We like to play with sticky goo
And we have a little secret too,
We have very, very smelly poo.

Sometimes we breathe fire and ice,
Other times we try to be nice,
We like to keep lots and lots of pet mice.

My friends and I sleep all day
But at night that's when we come out to play,
So beware, naughty children
Because you are our prey.

Goodbye for now,
But always look around,
We don't just live underground.

Savanna Rose Johnson (9)
Bracken Leas Primary School, Brackley

Friendly Flurry

Flurry was born on the moon
To sing a nice, peaceful tune.
She had no fear,
No matter where they were.
Flurry always was good
And just ate all her food.
She always was nice
And gave advice.
When she had trouble,
She would see her double.
If she was sad, she would feel bad.
She listened to the stereo and heard the radio.
If she had pain, she would complain.
When she fainted, someone painted.
When she would glide, she fell the tide.

Rachel Marie Baker (8)
Bracken Leas Primary School, Brackley

Ten Eyes

Ten Eyes came to Earth from Mars,
He saw Jupiter and a million stars.
He had two magnificent mouths
That were wider than a majestic mountain.
Ten Eyes had five knobbly noses
That could nip quite nastily.
He tried to say hello to people
But they all ran away
Because of his alarming appearance.
This made him super sad.
In the end, Ten Eyes got so sad
That he went from Earth to Mars.
He saw Venus and a million stars.

Esme Blurton (9)
Bracken Leas Primary School, Brackley

Zalfrid The Wimp

My name is Zalfrid, I am a one-eyed monster.
I'm short and fluffy and have a pet called Sydney.
I like doing space walks around the planet of Mars.
I fly there in my spaceship, the awesome Clop 1.
I also go to Pluto with my best friend, Budo.
We go there to visit our other friend, Pudo.
We like going on adventures, it's really great fun
but we often get scared and have to fly home to
our mum.

Alex Bundy (9)
Bracken Leas Primary School, Brackley

Cheeki The Fluff Ball

Cheeki is as fluffy as a cloud
with pink bubblegum fluff
and a lovely flower crown,
playing Monster Whizz with her friends,
laughing and giggling along the way.
Cheeki is as fluffy as a cloud,
now she waves goodbye to her friends
and straightens her crown.
"Turn that frown upside down," said one
of her friends.
"We will see you tomorrow!"
And that was the end!

Lucy Creek (9)
Bracken Leas Primary School, Brackley

My Monster Fuzzy

My monster, Fuzzy, is cute,
She likes to eat fruit,
No one knows why she's shy
Or why she cries.

My monster, Fuzzy, is pink,
She smells of lavender and doesn't stink.
Her hair is furry
And is very, very swirly.

My monster, Fuzzy, has fangs,
She plays the drums with big loud bangs.

My monster, Fuzzy, is sweet,
The nicest monster you'll ever meet.

Elizabeth Braker (9)
Bracken Leas Primary School, Brackley

Monster In The House

There's a monster in the house
It is bigger than a mouse
I shiver in the coldness
Whenever I see his boldness
He hides under my bed
And bends his big head
He sharpens his big teeth
And says, "I want my food!"
I whisper, "Ssh, go to bed
And don't let me see your head!"
He ducked under the bed once more
And I soon could hear him snore.

Scarlett Sellick (8)
Bracken Leas Primary School, Brackley

My Best Friends

Melly is very smelly and friendly
to the people next door
but when he chats he's a bore
but nonetheless, he likes apple cores.

Melly's favourite treat is cookie,
he loves sharing with his best friend, Brookie.
He is a Wookie and is very mucky.

Although Melly is smelly
and Brookie is a mucky Wookie
I still love them because they are my best friends.

Emily White (8)
Bracken Leas Primary School, Brackley

Fluffycorn

He's sunrise yellow with purple eyes,
he has to power to magnetise.
If he lifts you in the air
you have to pretend you just don't care.
He will let you down with a gentle bump
and on your head will be no lump.
Just smile and wave your hand in the air
then run a mile and check your hair.
If it's yellow you've been got
by Sunrise Fluffycorn that laughs a lot.

Bethany Williams (8)

Bracken Leas Primary School, Brackley

Octicute

Octicute, Octicute
You are so cute.
Octicute, Octicute
In your pink suit.

Octicute, Octicute
You are so pretty.
Octicute, Octicute
As soft as a kitty.

Octicute, Octicute
You are so fluffy.
Octicute, Octicute
But not so toughy!

Octicutc, Octicute
You're my monster friend.
Octicute, Octicute
My bestie till the end.

Ella Morris (9)
Bracken Leas Primary School, Brackley

Terrible Tiggy

Terrible Tiggy loved her food.
Without her food she would be in a bad mood.
The most favourite food was yellow slime
which meant she had stinky feet all the time.
All the monsters thought she was snobby
except for one of her friends who went by the
name of Bobby.
They would go underground on lots of adventures.
One day they even found Grandpa searching for
his dentures.

Ellie Mae Hughes (9)

Bracken Leas Primary School, Brackley

Blob The Friendly Monster

Blob lived in the sewer.
He loved to make friends like Fang.
Blob was a friendly monster.
One day he went through the woods
Then a boy came along
And dug a hole and put a net over it.
Blob looked slimy, bobbly and gooey.
Blob got caught in the trap and he said, "I am
friendly."
The boy made a monster friend.
Blob was happy with his new friend.

Phoebe Marron (9)

Bracken Leas Primary School, Brackley

Venom And Poison

Venom was on his way
To scare all the innocent away.
What he saw was unbelievable,
It was extremely shockable.
They looked exactly the same,
Except they both had a different name.
They fought off heroes pretty quickly,
With a big gun and very happily.
Venom is good friends with Poison,
It certainly isn't an illusion.

Niamh Cummings (8)

Bracken Leas Primary School, Brackley

Naughty

I'm a tall and naughty monster.
I'm an inky, little monster.
I always get up to mischief every single day.

I always get up to trouble.
Mischief follows me around.
Being naughty is my thing.

I'm never kind to others.
I don't like being nice.
A monster through and through.

Josh Taylor (9)
Bracken Leas Primary School, Brackley

Here Comes Treble

He is big, he is scary,
He is very, very hairy.
Nobody likes him in his group
Because he has smelly poop.
People who teased him were mean and nasty,
It only happened after a Cornish pasty.
When anyone saw him coming
They would all start running.
Uh oh, who's that rebel?
Here comes Treble!

Tom Cadden (9)

Bracken Leas Primary School, Brackley

Monsters Everywhere

Monsters, monsters everywhere
Monsters, monsters, slimy hair
Monsters, monsters, big green eyes
Monsters, monsters, "Boo...! Surprise!"
Monsters, monsters under my bed
Monsters, monsters in my head.
Monsters, monsters in my drawer.
Monsters, monsters... *Roar!*

Ellie Lauren Prescott Wright (9)
Bracken Leas Primary School, Brackley

Freya The Fluffyball

Freya the fluffy keep-fit monster
Who jogs around Pluto every morning.

She has black, fiery eyes and a freaky mouth
But is as friendly as a flamingo and as jumpy as a
frog.

With pink and yellow fuzzy stripes
She zooms around Pluto as fast as a ferret.

Isla Wakefield (9)

Bracken Leas Primary School, Brackley

The Monster Called Jerry

Jerry is a friendly monster.
He was born in a forest.
He has brown, fluffy fur.
He has green, grassy eyes.
He has thousands of furry friends
And likes playing tag.
He is like a cheetah in speed.
His favourite subject at school is of course English.

Harley King (9)
Bracken Leas Primary School, Brackley

Snadragious

Snadragious is a fierce and frightening beast
Who comes out at night in search of a feast.
He is part dragon with spikes on his head,
And part snake, all scaly and red.
Strangest of all he's got an ankylosaurus tail,
It looks like a club; round and pale.

Annabel Kibble (9)

Bracken Leas Primary School, Brackley

Zip

His name is Zip
And he runs at a clip.

He gives wonderful cuddles
But always gets in a muddle.

He's as cheeky as Horrid Henry
And as fluffy as a bunny.

He is frightened of a pineapple
Because it spikes his delicate skin.

Charlotte Brawn (8)
Bracken Leas Primary School, Brackley

My Monster

Some people think monsters are enormous,
Even as big as a stegosaurus,
But the one under my bed
Is only as big as my head.

Some people think monsters eat boys
And make a terrible noise,
Mine wouldn't eat me
And is as kind as can be.

Grace Sharpe (9)
Bracken Leas Primary School, Brackley

Monsters

Monsters, monsters, where do they live?
Under my bed or in a crib.

Monsters, monsters, who could they be?
Disguised as your friend or as a tree.

Yet I'm still sat here thinking of what they can be.
Maybe as a mother or like you and me.

Connor Cooper (9)

Bracken Leas Primary School, Brackley

Monsters, Monsters

Monsters, monsters
Scary and hairy
Monsters, monsters
Giant and intelligent
Monsters, monsters
Smelly and jolly
Monsters, monsters
Furry and fierce
Monsters, monsters
Tiny and tall
Monsters, monsters
You scare us all.

Amy Bishop (8)
Bracken Leas Primary School, Brackley

Monsters Are...

Monsters are hairy, scary and rude.
Monsters are greedy and picky about food.
Monsters are noisy, loud and brave.
Monsters are stinky and live in a cave.
Monsters are tall with really brown nails.
Monsters are gross and like eating snails.

Amelia Sharpe (9)
Bracken Leas Primary School, Brackley

Dear Jimbob

Dear Jimbob,
You live under my bed,
Your colour is red,
You pick the dreams,
That fill my head,
You snooze during the day,
So you can keep me safe at night,
No matter the size of my worries,
You can always put them right.

Harrison Rhys Wilkins (8)
Bracken Leas Primary School, Brackley

Orange Ozzy

Orange Ozzy likes going over oval obstacles
And under upside-down umbrellas.
He devours orange juice, jelly and jam.
However, if he doesn't devour juice, jelly and jam...
He goes green, gooey and grumpy!

Callum Platt (9)
Bracken Leas Primary School, Brackley

Stich

He is a smelly monster with rough, scaly skin,
who has no friends because of his dreadful
manners and bad breath.
He lives in a dark and gloomy cave with spiders
and bats.
Stich is the scariest monster around.

Ollie Hirons (9)
Bracken Leas Primary School, Brackley

Bobby

Bobby is a monster who lives in the park.
He only comes out to play when it's dark.
Bobby likes to play with his friends and has
a kind heart.
Bobby's glad that he lives in the park.

Maddie Fairey (9)
Bracken Leas Primary School, Brackley

The Polka-dot Monster

I am a polka-dot monster
I look like a lobster
I am a famous boxer
I love playing soccer
I used to be a doctor
But now I am a robber
And I melt in water.

Batiste De Oliveira (8)
Bracken Leas Primary School, Brackley

The Monster

My name is Haa
I eat road tar.

I scare lots of people.
I live on top of a steeple.

I come out at night.
I give you a fright.

Thomas Ansell (9)
Bracken Leas Primary School, Brackley

The Growler

The Growler looks hairy and scary
And can be incredibly lairy,
But really and truly
He isn't unruly,
He prefers dressing up as a fairy!

Reuben Adkins (8)
Bracken Leas Primary School, Brackley

Fluffy

Fluffy is a cloud and he loves being loud.
He is having so much fun that he can barely run.
He never really goes to bed
Even if he is red.
He loves laughing and he never stops partying.
One of his friends is Dave
But you might need to tell him to behave.
Another friend is Bobby
And he likes to pretend to be a monkey.
Another friend is Jeff
But he would like to be a ref.
One's Jake and he has a teddy called Blake.
We've also got James
Who loves playing games.
There's Billy who is kind of silly,
He never stops playing even if it's raining.
He likes candy because it could come in handy.
I've got to run because this poem is done!

Oliver Trimble (8)
Grendon CE Primary School, Grendon

Cuddles And Snuggles

Hi, my name is Cuddles
I have a friend called Snuggles.
Together we travel the world.
This time it is Egypt to watch the camels stroll by.
We help each other through the sandy desert.
I live in Greece.
We stay away from the spiky cactus
So we don't get prickled.
We may look different
But actually, we are the same inside
So get on my back for a ride.
Don't be worried or look back
Be happy, don't be down,
Help others if they need, don't frown.
Smile, don't do it the other way round
This is me every day, helping others to play
Even when I am away.
Bye for now 'cause this poem is done
... Don't be like The Fiend.

Hannah Wright (8)
Grendon CE Primary School, Grendon

The Story Of Fuzzy

Hi, my name is Fuzzy,
My friends call me Buzzy
And I have a friend called JJ,
He has a toy named Mama
And he likes doing the nae nae.
My bestest friend is called Fluf,
Sometimes she messes up,
Also, my friend named Red,
He is pretty and red.

I have wings and I can fly sky high.
I'm fluffy but I'm not scruffy.
I'm dotty and I'm spotty.
When I dance I'm in a trance.
I might need to run
Because this poem is done!

Sophie McCloy (9)
Grendon CE Primary School, Grendon

The Story Of Fluf

Hi, I'm Fluf,
I can live on a cheese puff.

I have a friend called Mama,
He has a toy named JJ
And loves to do the nae nae.

I go to parties,
End up being happy
But everybody else is in a nappy.

My best friend is called Fuzzy
And she wants to be a bunny.

I might need to run
Because the poem is done.

Grace McCloy (9)
Grendon CE Primary School, Grendon

I'm Huggle!

Hi, my name is Huggle
And I like to snuggle!

I like to sing and swing
But I don't fling!
I like to dance all day and all night,
Come on everybody, let's take flight!
My heart is as light as a feather,
Come on, let's do it together!
I better swim because you know
I don't like to fling!

Holly Philo (9)
Grendon CE Primary School, Grendon

Angry

There was a monster called Angry.
Angry likes to play.
If you make him mad he'll turn grey.
Angry likes animals to eat.
Now I can tell that you don't want to meet.
Angry isn't clever
And he's never going to come out of his cave.
So if you want to meet this horrible monster...
You're lucky!

Cecily Bamford (8)
Grendon CE Primary School, Grendon

Phantom

Phantom is a ghost, he is very shy with floating
hands and can turn invisible.
He wants an adventure but he is too shy.
He is as shy as a hidden book.
He tried and tried and finally succeeded.
Then he set off very carefully.
He went to a haunted forest that he did not know
then he walked into a house.
Then he noticed it...
It was all haunted!
"I have to get out of this forest and the house too,"
said Phantom.
First he got out of the house,
the path had disappeared.
He found a map
then he followed it all the way out.
Suddenly a monster appeared, he was super
strong but Phantom faced him.
He turned his hands invisible and sent him to
shake him so that's what they did.
Then nearly every monster looked up to him.

James Atkins (8)
Hayfield Cross CE School, Kettering

My Monster Friend

On a dark and stormy night,
where nothing was bright,
except my flickering little light,
which was shaped like a kite.

I was sleeping peacefully,
when a loud crash broke the silence,
I peered under my bed
and saw an adorable, shy creature.

She was three inches tall,
which is really small.

For a while I stared, I stared,
nervously I stared, nervously and excitedly,
so there she lived under my bed
until one night she said, "Come with me."

Away we went under my bed
to a world I haven't seen,
it looked like a dream.

Then she called and something came from
the distance,
a unicorn came singing my name.

We clambered aboard and there we were,
flying across the land of my imagination.

Then the unicorn landed, it was time to go,
a few minutes later, there I was,
once again in my bed,
The creature spoke, "By the way my name is Cutie
Pie and it's time for me to say goodbye."

Eva Katherine Davies (9)
Hayfield Cross CE School, Kettering

I'm A Troublemaker Flossie

For this day I'm going to the pool,
Late at night that would be cool
"Okay that sounds okay but not tonight.
Sleep tight and you'll get a fright."
So he sneaked out without a doubt,
In the swimming pool he drank all the water out.
End this now but I should... *Burppp!*
Follow me and you can have some tea.
Long way home, the people had sore legs
And now he slept till 12.30am.
Soon he never knew, it was on the news
He was sorry for the chaos and the cow moos.
"I'm sorry Beyoncé, I didn't make your day.
End this and you will be on the double
I will never make trouble again."
I'm better than before, I'm a model.
So keep me in your hands and I'll keep you safe.

Kaeley Naughton (8)
Hayfield Cross CE School, Kettering

Phantom

A long time ago in a galaxy far, far away,
Caramel a monster Gunggung lived.

Baboom, baboom!
Caramel crashlanded on epic Earth.
The sign was fine!

It made a hut
But it was out of power.
In his garden he only had a flower.

Boom, kaboom!
Caramel saw a ship zoom.

Caramel said, "What is that ship?"
And, "I don't know that guy a bit!"

"Oh what's your name?"
"Phantom."
"That's a shame, I'm a Gunggung!"

There's some monsters,
"I'll bet them," and he did.
"Let's make friends," and they did.

Sebastian Burton (7)
Hayfield Cross CE School, Kettering

One Christmas

One Christmas morning, a long time ago,
I opened a present all wrapped in a bow.
Mum and Dad said, "We didn't get you this."
It was squishy, friendly and adorable too.
It was a monster, as kind as you.
"My name is Squidgy," he said in a gentle voice.
I fell in love with him instantly,
I simply had no choice.
My monster opened my next present,
It was a Rolls Royce.
The holiday went and was gone
And Squidgy was still with me.
On the first day back Squidgy had sneaked
Into my bag.
Me and my friend played a game called tag.
I looked in my bag and saw him, squidgier than
usual.
"Why are you here?"
Squidgy never answered.

Amy Roche (9)
Hayfield Cross CE School, Kettering

Poison Dart

Poison Dart lives in space
He was born in a volcano
He was coming down for a big race
That's if he could tie his lace.

If you touch him he spits out poison
Then he turns invisible and shapeshifts
It's like nothing has hit you.

He crashed in the shed
So I've been told by Ned
Bang, bang, crash, bang, crash, kaboom!
He is like a secret terror
And mysterious.

It was like a bull in a china shop
It's time to say goodbye
He said he would come back another day.

But this time he would win the race...
In space, goodbye for now Poison Dart.

Imogen Eve Hollwey (9)
Hayfield Cross CE School, Kettering

Bone Killer's Hunt!

Bone Killer, Bone Killer, Bone Killer's hunt,
He's a teleporter, a murderer,
A terrifying skeleton.
Long ago he wanted to be president
But now all he does is think of the present.
He also does hunting.
"Murderer!" the critics say,
He doesn't care for he has spoiled
Someone's day!

Bone Killer, Bone Killer, Bone Killer's hunt,
He's a teleporter, a murderer,
A terrifying skeleton,
"Killer, killer, we need to run away!
Oh no... he's here,
I'll never see the light of day!
Argh!"
"See you in your nightmares!"

Jack Anthony Moreton (9)
Hayfield Cross CE School, Kettering

A School Day With A Monster

My monster is called Scwibbles,
Looks more like a cat's hairball,
Soft like candyfloss,
Except he doesn't taste nice,
Today I took him to school,
Down the bumpy road,
Hoping that he wouldn't fall,
As we sat down Scwibbles broke the chair,
Then blamed me,
Then I shouted, "That's not fair!"
After, we went to lunch
Scwibbles threw the food around
And stuck mash potato to the ceiling.
At playtime we skipped,
Scwibbles tripped.
He was hurt real bad,
When we got home we lay in bed,
Waiting to be fed.

Alexis Jane Sumpter (9)
Hayfield Cross CE School, Kettering

Flexy The Flexible Monster

At gymnastics one day there was a new arrival,
it was a spotty, stretchable and flexible monster.

She was different to all of the others
about six foot two.
She did not escape from anywhere like the zoo,
even her family looked like her too.

She was good at lots of stuff like the other people,
floor, beams, driving cars!
Finally she was swinging on the bars,
lots of people said she looked like a bat from
Mars.

At the end of the session they all said,
"I wish we could all be monsters instead!"

Sienna Ward (8)
Hayfield Cross CE School, Kettering

The Hamburger Monster!

In a restaurant there was a family.
A racket came from inside the kitchen.
Slowly a creature that looked like a hamburger
with a face and legs rose from the side of
the counter.
He yelled and when they saw its teeth they raced
out of the building.
Why were they running from a hamburger?

He was a sneaky, careless, mischievous burger
known as the Horrific Hamburger.
"Where has he come from?" the people asked.
Till Farmer Bill saw him and ate him.
This was the end of him, or was it?

Annabel Fiddy (9)
Hayfield Cross CE School, Kettering

Monster School

I'm a fuzzy monster
Who's really kind and sweet.
I'm kind of shy
But we could make friends in a beat.
I'm a fuzzy monster
And I'm going to school
With my best friend, Georgy,
He's good at fighting fools!
I feel kind of safe now,
Nobody can harm me.
I don't know what to do
Since the only human thing I've ever used is a Wii!
Things are way better,
The day's been really fun,
I really hate to say this
But the day is done and done!

Tireni Owolabi (8)
Hayfield Cross CE School, Kettering

58

My Friendly Friend

My friendly friend is a monster who I made up in my head.
I called it Picmin.
Picmin came alive and I cried, "I've got a magic monster pet."
I went to the park and she barked in the night light.
On Wednesday we went on an adventure and we saw a unicorn.
My fluffy, cute, funny, wonderful monster rode her beautiful back.
"It was like a dream!" she shouted in a laugh.
Today I said this again.
"My friendly friend is a monster who I made up in my head."

Lauren Large (9)
Hayfield Cross CE School, Kettering

A Lightning Day

Today I went to school
to find it gushing with rain the size of pools,
lightning bigger than I had ever seen before.
An evil monster appeared,
an evil and petrifying monster appeared,
an evil, petrifying and ferocious monster appeared.
Suddenly he walked towards me,
"Let's make friends!" the monster said.
"And my name is Lightning Strike."
We went to the beach.
Lightning Strike touched the water and he
disappeared.
I hope he comes back again.

Oscar Burton (9)
Hayfield Cross CE School, Kettering

The Monster Under My Bed

When I was in bed I looked under the bed
Because something was making a racket.
Out came a head as pink as a rose.
Its name was Nice Lolly and it looked like an ice
lolly.

When I got out of bed, waiting to be fed
He followed me downstairs and everywhere I went.

I tried my best to get out of his mess
With the cute, fluffy and cheerful thing following
me.

When I got back into bed
He went back under but the next day he was gone.

Eva Johnson (9)
Hayfield Cross CE School, Kettering

I Saw A Monster

I went to the park with my friends
and had a strange smell in my nose.
It was a sticky, smelly monster.
My friends ran off but I stayed and joined the fun.
I said, "Monster oh monster, do you have any friends?"
The monster whispered back to me and said, "No!"
"Monster, oh monster, what's your name?"
"Flat Jack," he replied.
"What a very cute name!"
After that day we finally became friends.

Chloe Large (9)
Hayfield Cross CE School, Kettering

Monster At School

On the way to school,
I met a little monster,
Its fur was rainbow
And its name was Unimon.

It came along with me,
It caused lots of mischief,
It scared everyone at break
And it escaped from class.

I got angry with her
And she left straight away.

I don't think I'll see her again,
She's long gone.

She left with terrible rage
And then she got put in a cage.

Isla Coe (8)
Hayfield Cross CE School, Kettering

Gummy Bears Eat You!

One boiling hot day, there was a group of girls.
"Don't go into the forest," their mum warned.
The opposite happened.
The girls played in the forest, *crash!*
There was a colossal, petrifying and selfish gummy bear, Chaos!
He stole their cakes, their dolls and ate them in one big gulp!
"You eat gummy bears but gummy bears can eat you!" he warned.
Home they ran.
But what will he do next?

Amelia Woodcock (9)
Hayfield Cross CE School, Kettering

Monster Queen!

One day, on the way to school
I met a monster who was furry,
His eyes were very blurry.
I took him to school,
His name was Mike.
My monster was very kind.
When I got home my monster went to my room.
Mike played with the broom.
Me and Monster went to see the Queen.
We saw Unimon.
She said we could sleep round her house,
So we did.
We went home.

Noah Sturges (7)
Hayfield Cross CE School, Kettering

The Fluff Ball

There was once a monster who was fluffy and funny.

There was once a monster who came from excellent England.

She loved having seas to seize the bad.

She loved having marvellous McDonald's and seeing Little Mix.

She had only one friend called Sophie.

Fluffball, cute, fluffy, fuzzy and funny.

She loved going in the Wailing Woods.

This time she saw a united dragon.

Sophie Ireson-Vaughan (9)
Hayfield Cross CE School, Kettering

Slobbery Nightmare

I was wandering around in the desert mound
and I came across a terrible sight.
It had an awful eye and a slimy tongue.
If it was my imagination then I'm thinking in the
dead of night, *I will ignite.*
If that's not enough, well, it's best enough.
Well I will hide in a pie.
It may not smell me,
but it does definitely know me!

William Cruttwell (9)
Hayfield Cross CE School, Kettering

On The Way To The River

On the way to the river, I saw a snake under a bush.
I looked under the bush.
"It's a monster!" I said.
I stayed calm.

But then it rolled out and looked at me.
It was a shy creature.
She climbed trees, she jumped in the rivers.
And I went with her too.
But then it was time to go home
And she came with me too.

Catherine Ward (8)
Hayfield Cross CE School, Kettering

My Favourite Day

At home in my bedroom, there was a loud noise.
I looked under my bed,
I dangled my head,
It was a monster!
Her name was Fluff Pot,
She was as blue as the sky.
And she could shoot lasers
Out of her eyes.
She was pretty, fluffy and cute,
She was amazing.
"Shh, my mum will hear
And I will get in double trouble!"

Brianna Starsmore (8)
Hayfield Cross CE School, Kettering

On The Way To School

One day on the way to school
I saw a little monster in a holly tree.
I picked him up and took him to school,
I wanted to show and tell him
But he finally said a word,
He said, "My name is Darkymon."
He went to sleep, I put him in my bag.
I got to school,
The children were playing, shouting, running.
Darkymon woke up.

Jude Ennis Drury (7)
Hayfield Cross CE School, Kettering

Fluffy's Adventure!

One day there was a monster, orange, fluffy and cute.
When it was walking in the forest,
it saw an old leather boot.
It heard a rustle in a hedge
and a bustle on a ledge.
It looked in a hedge
and there it saw a monster with really sharp claws.
They made a decision to be friends
and their favourite thing to do was practice division.

Joel Smith (8)
Hayfield Cross CE School, Kettering

Fluffy And Me

On the way home I met...
A monster gentle, hairy and cute.
She was about six foot two,
She was cute,
She was really cute,
She was really, really cute!
Fluffy said, "I want to go home!"
She was as sad as ever.
When we got home she disappeared.
I asked, "Where is Fluffy?"
But she was gone.

Holly Greasley (9)
Hayfield Cross CE School, Kettering

The Evil Squad

The goodies came and they brought the Octo
Samurai!
He was the worst, he used a splat roller as a
motorbike.
He charged at me and then I evolved into Magmar!
Then me, DanTDM 3000 and Deathy jumped into
the cannon and we flew
as a cow said, "Moo!"
Then we punched the Earth
and *boom!* We destroyed the Earth!

Callum Brooks (8)
Hayfield Cross CE School, Kettering

Adi And Me

There was a thing under my bed,
Under my head a creature read,
A story, a soothing story,
A story to be read.

He was a well-mannered monster,
A mischievous monster,
As cheeky as can be,
He was an adorable monster,
He was a squishy monster
And he was friends with me!

Abi Daly (8)
Hayfield Cross CE School, Kettering

I Saw A Monster

I saw a monster,
Hairy and fat,
He was holding a bat
And he was going to smash.
Just at that moment, there was a bash!
We all turned our heads and there was a crash!
Just then the monster knocked me over
And at that moment he jumped in the trash
And was never to be seen again.

Elliot Nicholls (9)
Hayfield Cross CE School, Kettering

Little Friend

Once I met a monster
With all its furry fur
It had purple fur and a golden patterned purse
To spare the mercy of Blur.

After we stared we had a friendly relationship.
The next day I saw she was not there.
I sat there with a tear of sadness,
My friend was gone with gladness.

Lucy Terry (8)
Hayfield Cross CE School, Kettering

Sparkles

S parkles went to visit the Queen
P rince Harry was there too
A big furry cat as well
R eliable friends were there
K een to play in the garden
L oving the day
E veryone had fun
S parkles did too!

Scarlett Breakell (7)
Hayfield Cross CE School, Kettering

Meothra

When I was in the park
I saw a shy, cute and cuddly creature.
My friends thought it was a cat or a bat.
We watched it as its eyes glimmered like gems.
I took it to school and we had fun together
And then I took it home.

Lily Sales (8)
Hayfield Cross CE School, Kettering

Me And Fuzzy

F riendly, fuzzy friend
U ndoubtedly the best there is
Z ooming around my bedroom
Z igzagging with a zest for life
Y oung, little Fuzzy, she will always be there for me.

Skye Weatherley (8)
Hayfield Cross CE School, Kettering

Fluff

F riendly, little Fluff,
L ovely, long-lasting best friend,
U nderstanding the problems to help,
F riendship that never breaks,
F unny, favourite Fluff.

Neriah Angela Goodream-Wilson (8)
Hayfield Cross CE School, Kettering

Monster Poetry

Monster, monster, monster poetry.
Monster, monster giggles and fun.
Monster, monster, monster poetry.
Monster rhymes that tickle your tum.

Monster, monster, monster poetry.
Tiny, cute, fluffy and mini.
Monster, monster, monster poetry.
Very small and very skinny.

Monster, monster, monster poetry.
Monster likes to play hide-and-seek.
Monster, monster, monster poetry.
Monster hard to find so I peek.

Monster, monster, monster poetry.
Monster, monster, full of great joy.
Monster, monster, monster poetry.
Monster, monster, not just my toy.

Levi Nelson (8)
Irthlingborough Junior School, Irthlingborough

The Dark Destroyer

Beyond the summit of Suffer,
Where fear itself surrendered,
Its home seemed stuck in the past,
As long as time remembered.

A single eye held its hideous glare,
Its teeth as sharp as steel,
Claws exposed like daggers,
For it wanted to reveal
Those foolish enough to enter receive,
The invincible opponent Death,
When accepting your new fate,
It would pause your final breath,
All terrifying arms extended,
To prevent any possible raids,
Its body was the colour of the cosmos,
Its face wounded by the battles it made.

Freddie Nicklin (11) & Zak Swinton
Irthlingborough Junior School, Irthlingborough

Bedtime Freaks

B e aware, he will frighten you,

E verywhere he'll go boo.

D o you wonder if there's any monsters under your bed?

T ime to close your eyes,

I n the sun he fries.

M axle comes out at night,

E ven when you're tucked up tight.

F urry creatures creeping around,

R un away from Maxle.

E very night he will come

A nd give you bad dreams.

K ind monsters don't go to school,

S o be good and forget them (if you can).

Saoirse Gibbard (9)
Irthlingborough Junior School, Irthlingborough

Three Head Horror!

Beyond this planet far away,
On Mars monsters lurk,
People wonder who are they,
Just like an ambush in Dunkirk.

What are they? What are they?
Nobody knows.
What are they? What are they?
Who will know!

People set off to search,
But never come back,
Everybody knew what lurks,
In the pitch-black sky!

Wings that flap, arms that whack,
Eyes as red as blood!

Oliver Andrews (10) & Thomas Ritchings

Irthlingborough Junior School, Irthlingborough

No One Likes The Dark

Bright light, bright light.
Monsters are afraid of the bright light.
They search and search as far as they can see,
but they can't find any dark as you can see.

Dark, dark, glorious dark.
The monsters love the dark so much they can
scream.
They sleep in the day and wake in the night.
The dark is beautiful and light is hurtful.

Keira Thomas (8)
Irthlingborough Junior School, Irthlingborough

Friendly Fred

There's a monster under my bed,
He's called Friendly Fred.
But if I don't call him Ned,
He'll mess up my bed.

One day after school
I saw a terrible sight.
Friendly Fred had smashed my bed.
I thought about where I was going to sleep,
Before I had a peep,
To see if anyone was there,
On the stair.

Miley Louise Jackson (9)
Irthlingborough Junior School, Irthlingborough

The Creeping Monster

Monsters black
Demons fly
We will eat you
So don't you cry
We will sing you a lullaby
So don't be scared
Papa is nice
So we'll give you a fright
We creep at night
We scare you in the daylight
So witches fly on brooms
So we swing
We will be free
Now you're dead,
He, he, he!

Lana Eldridge (9)
Irthlingborough Junior School, Irthlingborough

The Monster Stomp

If you want to be a monster
Well now's your time to shine
'Cause everyone's doing the monster cheer.
Just wave your arms and stomp your feet,
Stretch your arms, stretch your feet,
Touch the ground
'Cause we're doing the monster cheer.
Monster cheer, oh, oh, oh yeah!

Becky Bushby (9)
Irthlingborough Junior School, Irthlingborough

Hello Monster

Hello monster
How are you doing?
Goodbye monster
See you again

Hello monster
How long have we known each other?
Goodbye monster
See you later.

Hello monster
It's been so long
Goodbye monster
Never again.

Katie Boardman (10)
Irthlingborough Junior School, Irthlingborough

The Monster Poem

M onsters are mean
O bnoxiousness will take over
N asty as can be
S tinky as rotten cheese
T hey will kill every soul
E veryone will get eaten
R oam the whole galaxy
S o beware of the monsters.

Alexander Barley (8)
Irthlingborough Junior School, Irthlingborough

Pinky The Monster

Pinky the monster is happy and bright,
She will stay up almost all night
And she won't bite!

Pinky the monster is always happy,
She never lets sadness get the best of her!

Natalie Robinson (9)
Irthlingborough Junior School, Irthlingborough

Planet Kon

O ver the sun, past the meteorite belt

V icious rocks and UFOs go past.

E ven though it's a long journey you still get there

R unning to get to Planet Kon. When you arrive

L ord Kon gets into a ship with Khan Kish.

O ver to Planet Shroom to see Drag Clops.

R unning to see the fight of the lords.

D ying with hope that Lord Kon will win.

K on won the fight and earned a trophy.

O n that day it was a day to remember.

N ow Lord Kon is an overlord.

Kai Ethan Filbee (8)

Overstone Park School, Northampton

Crime World

This is a world where a rhyme saves Time.
We want to destroy Time,
with a crime,
but Time is a giant shapeshifting mime,
so it's going to be hard to beat Time,
with a crime.
Time also takes the form of a chime.
Then transforms into a deadly mime.
I broke Time's fine line.
Time used a chime rhyme.
I died but Time used a rhyme and saved me.
Me and Time became friends.

Jaylen Aaron Isaac Ferdinand (10)
Overstone Park School, Northampton

Lovely's Life

One day there was a creature called Lovely.
Lovely was three years old.
Her birthday was on the 1st of November.
She was very short, pretty and spotty.
She was a clever creature.
One day she played the game Who's Who?
She won and sometimes she lost.
She moved to Spain.
She was happy.

Lauryn Morgan (9)
Overstone Park School, Northampton

Days With Fuzzcorn

Days with Fuzzcorn are always such fun,
We go to the park to have a little run.
Together we play and laugh all day,
Because Fuzzcorn is always special in my day.
Fuzzcorn is gentle, caring and kind,
After playing all day long in a park we find
Fuzzcorn's cousin Fluff who is stuck in a box.
So Fuzzcorn takes Fluff out to play with our friendly
fox.
Days with Fuzzcorn are always such fun,
And ever so special because there's so much to be
done!
I can't wait for tomorrow, for more laughter and
play
Because Fuzzcorn is always special in my day.

Patricia Alfaro Pereira (8)
Stimpson Avenue Academy, Northampton

Me And My Monster

On the way back from school
I met a monster round and blue,
He was as blue as the ocean.
He wasn't lost but he wasn't happy
Until I asked him, "What's the problem?"
He answered back saying, "I have no friends."
But then I asked him, "Can I be your friend?"
He said, "Yes," merrily and cheerfully
And then we went happily.
We went to my house to ask my mum.
If we could go to the park and have some fun.
And then we asked if we could bring a kite
To have some fun.
And then we said, "We'll be back in a quick time."
We rode the swings happily and joyfully
And then we flew the kite
After a while my mum called us back.
So then we started to go.
After walking for a while I saw him walking
So we hid and gave her a stunning surprise
After that we said goodbye

And off he went to his home sweet home.
On the way back from school
I bumped into a monster.
I saw that he was sad and mad.
And I asked him, "What's the problem?
What's your name?"
"My name is Googly."
I took him home.

Ummur Ali (8)
Stimpson Avenue Academy, Northampton

My Monster Milly Met Tilly

My monster is called Milly
And is super-duper silly.

She went to Majorca
Where she met a walker.

His name was Floss
And he was the boss.

Now let's move on to food,
Not be a chicken and brood.

Milly's favourite food is bird,
With a little lemon curd.

When she went back to Sweetland
She met a brass band.

In it was Tilly,
Who was very, very frilly.

They went to a fair,
To watch a bear.

They went on swingboats
In fat, woolly coats.

Now it's time to say goodbye,
So have some apple pie.

By the way
It's as bright as the sun.

Faith Bainger (8)
Stimpson Avenue Academy, Northampton

The Cute Beast

The beast was born at mid-dawn,
near a gigantic foghorn.
He was near a shed,
which was red,
like a broken bed.
It was dark and he tried to bark.
Prickles is cute,
and loves parachutes.
Prickles always loves big tickles,
but he won't stop nicking pickles.

He loves Skittles, his favourite snack,
he tried grabbing it back.
At last he started to blast off,
cough, cough, cough!
Prickles ran out of food
and was in a bad mood.
So now he's on a mat,
sleeping in a hat
and fast asleep in a flat.

Fayez Ahmed (8)
Stimpson Avenue Academy, Northampton

Fluff's Day

In the park
I saw a monster called Fluff
With his best mate, Floss,
They were eating ice cream on the swing.

They were in Adventure Island.
After the park,
They went to a party,
They saw a funny monster,
He was super scruffy and really fluffy.

When they got home it was dark.
They started to shout and bark.
Then went outside and played catch.
It was a match.
The moon started to glow
And the sun would go.

When they went to bed
Fluff said, "I'm going to sleep. Goodnight"

James Lawford Braithwaite (7)
Stimpson Avenue Academy, Northampton

The Undiscovered Planet

One day when I was walking in town
A vast meteor came and hit the ground.
And when it hit the stony ground
It made the pavement nice and round.
On the meteor there was only one monster
With a mouldy plum.
He did not try to hide,
He just told me that he flew.
He walked around bends
Trying to make some new friends.
The monster told me its name
And it was Yracs Retsnom
And that he was the odd one out in his species.
I told him that my name was Rysees
And from then on we were best buddies.

Samuel Dwelly (9)

Stimpson Avenue Academy, Northampton

The Lab Experiment

Zhamba was born in a lab accident
when we tried to clone a dog.
This happened because one of the lab people
broke the most important cog.
Zhamba met me in a park
but all he would do was try to bark.
My marvellous monster makes me moan
but all I would do is just groan.
Zhamba tries to do backflips
and all he would do is break his hips.
Once I saw him on a swing,
he was destroying everything.
My monster is as colourful as a rainbow,
I will see him again tomorrow.

Zakk Carpenter (8)
Stimpson Avenue Academy, Northampton

My Marvellous Monster

I met my monster in my dreams
But she is not as nice as she seems.
She also likes eating yummy ice cream.
My monster is Furry,
She lives in Candyland
Where children are banned
And marshmallows are on the ground like snow.
We went to the park.
"Oh no, I hate the dark!"
Later on a firework started to blow
And Furry's eyes started to glow.
She is as furry as a furball,
My marvellous monster makes everyone moan,
Especially a monster called Joan.

Lola Akanmu (8)
Stimpson Avenue Academy, Northampton

Tilly And Her Friend Milly

Me and my monster hop in a rocket
Pop! We're off!
"Sweet Treat Land!" shouted Tilly cutely.
When we got there Tilly met Milly,
She was as cute as a baby bunny
And can even play the flute!
Together they went to the chewy chocolate and
sourly sweet shop.
"Yummy!" shouted Tilly.
They went to the fountain to eat.
Their tummies went funny.
When they'd finished Tilly said goodbye to Milly
That night they dreamed about gleams.

Emma McFadian (8)
Stimpson Avenue Academy, Northampton

My Fluffy Blob

Cuter Blob was born in a block.
She loves to dance but she never gets a chance.
Cuter is as cute as a mouse playing a flute.
She's as cute as a cat and as friendly as a rat.
She always loves to wear a hat.
She lives in California, but she doesn't have much fun.
She's not that keen about Milton Keynes.
Fluffy, friendly and fat,
I don't think you'll want to be like that.
Milton Keynes is filled with dreams,
But she's still not keen.

Areeba Islam (8)
Stimpson Avenue Academy, Northampton

Piper Buzz

One day, in New York City
A meteorite hit the Earth,
When it was coming down
The meteorite gave birth.
All the animals gave a big frown
And said they would make her drown.
As she was growing up
Lonely and with no friends,
She discovered that she could do magic.
When growing up as a furry monster,
She became a spy for other monsters,
Freezing time for the best,
Teaming up with a monster,
When she found some parties
She was filled with joy.

Emilija Balceraite (9)
Stimpson Avenue Academy, Northampton

Me And My Best Friend Monster

On the way to school I met a monster.
What I didn't know is that she was kind.
After school we went to the park.
We played all day and we heard a bird.
We played all day and we went home.
We looked at a book, we played tag,
hide-and-seek then we ate.
After, we went in into the garden and we played.
Then I asked my mum if the monster could stay
with me.
My mum said yes.
We were very happy about that.

Sandra Baltag (8)
Stimpson Avenue Academy, Northampton

The Chocomate Monster

The Chocomate was born in Candy Land.
He lived in a chocolate cave.
He was a very mean monster.
He wrecked Candy Land.
He broke down the gingerbread houses.
The village was in terror.
He was shooting chocolate out of turrets.
All the houses were coming down.
Everybody was running for their lives.
Chocomate was creeping carefully.
Chocomate was as tall as Mount Everest.

Shun Nyame (7)
Stimpson Avenue Academy, Northampton

Slimy

I was walking home from school
And I saw a gigantic, freaky creature.
Surprisingly he could talk.
His name was Bob Jingleberry.
He did a gigantic roar.
I was like, "Shut up!
You aren't scary Bob Jingleberry."
"Where are you?
You're too camouflaged, I can't see you."
I ducked in the bushes,
He never saw me spying.

Fin Shields (8)

Stimpson Avenue Academy, Northampton

The Shuzzy Monster

The Shuzzy was born on a volcano,
I met him at the beach.
I was swimming at the island pool,
He was buying some ice cream.
Everyone smiles at him,
He is nice and respectful to people.
His eyes are blue like the sky,
His skin is orange and fuzzy.
He is my little Shuzzy.
Shuzzy silently sleeps
When he silently, deeply falls into his dream.

Wiktoriq Seredynska (7)
Stimpson Avenue Academy, Northampton

My Happy Monster That's Tricky

The happy monster was born in the woods.
I met him in town by the stinky toilets.
He does tricks on people.
He makes funny hairstyles when people don't look very happy.
He acts crazy and he is lazy.
His skin colour is purple and he has green slime.
He likes slime but hates the taste of lime.
His skin is full of fuzz but doesn't like buzz.

Aida Vladi (8)

Stimpson Avenue Academy, Northampton

Oges The Monster

My name is Oges.

I am scary and hairy.

I was born in your nightmare and give such a fright.

You meet me in your nightmare.

I slowly creep into their bedrooms when they are asleep.

I am always there.

I creep into your bedroom and rip your teddies' heads off.

I go into your secret book and redo your secrets if you have some.

Raihana Kabeer (8)
Stimpson Avenue Academy, Northampton

The Beastly Creature

The beastly creature is running fast like a flash.
The beast was born in a creepy cave.
The beast is always mad and breaking things.
The beast is hideous.
The beast never gives up.
The beast never gets tired.
The beast always throws someone in the air.
The beast always damages houses.
He has brown skin and white horns.

Waseeur Rahman (8)

Stimpson Avenue Academy, Northampton

My Scary Monster

Mona was born in a park deep underground.
Whoever wakes her up will never ever come alive.
Mona is a gigantic monster
And she was spotted like a rotten rat playing
Very quickly on a big tower as tall as Big Ben.
This monster cannot only play quickly,
She can take your hand
And throw you in the air very quickly.

Mateusz Buczko (8)
Stimpson Avenue Academy, Northampton

The Beastly Creature

The beast really likes to feast.
He always goes east.
He always holds a bag and a flag.
The beast was born in Slimeville.
I met him outside my school.
Then I saw him run like a cheetah.
He saw me and ran to the miserable strangers.
He sneakily tiptoed into Slimeville.

Melchizedek N Poku (8)

Stimpson Avenue Academy, Northampton

My Monster Friend

One day I saw a monster in my garden.
It was hugging me lots and lots.
He drank Zoom and he got crazy!
He loved Zoom so he tried Zip.
He did not like it.
He is sneaky and creepy.
He likes blue and sticking glue.
He hates cows going moo!

Armands Mundiciems (8)
Stimpson Avenue Academy, Northampton

My Disaster Day With A Monster

One time I went to the science lab to get my laptop, then I saw my monster.
The monster was making an explosive volcano. When she put the baking soda in the volcano it exploded.
Boom!
She screamed.
She was cute and funny.

Ineta Alicia Ivanova (8)
Stimpson Avenue Academy, Northampton

The Evil Baby Devil

The baby devil was born in my dreams.
He is very bad but he is now very good.
He used to be bad but we trained him to help
people and save people.
He didn't have any friends but he does now
because he helped everyone.

Jake O'Connell (8)
Stimpson Avenue Academy, Northampton

My Monster Friend

Baby Big Feet was born in the English Channel.
I met him on a boat.
I was going to Germany.
He came with me.
He was well behaved and nice to people.
He was blue and pink.
He was cute and fuzzy.

Alex Plyoplev (8)

Stimpson Avenue Academy, Northampton

My Monster Friend

I met Pretty down the street
Near a tree she was reading a special book.
She was born in Italy.
Her family was born in Poland.
Pretty found a friend.
She behaved like a good girl.

Zayna Ali (8)
Stimpson Avenue Academy, Northampton

Sock Monster

Sock Monster will nick your socks
When you wake up because your feet are cold
no dog to keep them warm.
No cat to cuddle up to.
There's only one thing to keep you warm -
It's the Sock Monster!

Don't be scared.
He keeps the nightmares away.
He is there to protect you in every way.
Down in a corner.
There you are sent to bed.
Sock Monster is there.
No tears to fear.
He's your friend
and he will always be there
just like Mum and Dad.

Now you will never be lonely
because he is there under the bed.
He loves you with all his heart

even if you are bad
because you are one in a million,
just like a star.

Lillie Gallucci (10)
The Spires Academy, Great Billing

Ferpin

Your bedroom is like a dump,
Your monster just jumps and jumps.

You are always so bored,
On the shelf is where your monster is stored.

You're so very kind,
You and your monster combined.

Ferpin has two eyes.
Ferpin is so very wise.

The colour of your monster is rainbow.
He really likes to play with your yo-yo.

He is very useful with his pot of ink.
His favourite colour is pink.

You and Ferpin are better together.
You and Ferpin can live forever and ever.

Allan Holland (11)
The Spires Academy, Great Billing

Archie The Chocolate Monster!

He was born at my home,
That's how I met him in 2010.
He came from Irthlingborough.
Archie the chocolate monster likes eating
chocolate at 3am.
He scoffs it right in.
He likes to touch slime and other weird stuff such
as air fresheners.
The slime smells horrible but the car freshener
smells nice.
We like playing on my Xbox and on the laptop,
toy cars and slime and watching TV
and going to McDonald's with my parents.
I love him.

Alfie Green (10)
The Spires Academy, Great Billing

Roblox

When I first got Roblox I made a character,
Her name was Inkwell.
For her we smell of sweat
And she smells of ink and electric.
We play video games, chat with Chloe
And play scary games.
She can be happy, sad, excited
And sometimes a bit weird.
She likes scary games
But one day she randomly disappeared
And we heard something behind us...

Kayleigh Holmes (10)

The Spires Academy, Great Billing

The Destroyer Teddy Bear

The destroyer teddy bear has rips all over his body
And blood all over his teeth and has claws.
There is a blood splatter on his chest.
His fur is spiky, rough fur like a grizzly bear.
When you look into his eyes you turn to stone.
It creeps silently around your bedroom.
Beware! Lock your doors and windows for safety
From the destroyer teddy bear.

Finleigh Clewley (9)
The Spires Academy, Great Billing

Sweet Monsters

M olly wandered through the forest
O n her own after losing her friends.
N earing a house in a clearing.
S cary scientist lead her in
T old her to drink a glowing potion
E asily affecting her immediately. Claws sharpening, fur growing.
R escued by her monster friends, hiding together until the world ends.

Skye Louise Carter (11)

The Spires Academy, Great Billing

The Day The Monster Attacked!

It was a dark and stormy night.
All the villagers were inside.
Suddenly they saw a monster with dark blue hair.
He didn't need teeth because he was able to suck up humans.
He teleported into the house and slurped up an old, grey man.
Someone had a lightsaber and destroyed him.
He turned into thick, blue dust!

Logan Pegg (11)
The Spires Academy, Great Billing

Energy Monster

Downing monster juice every minute.
He bounces off the walls and ceilings.
Running crazily around his parents' massive
mansion.
Throwing a rugby ball as he goes.

Energy Monster never gets tired.
He's like a lightning bolt in a dark blue sky.
Louder than lightning.
Faster than The Flash.

Freddie Mayes (10)
The Spires Academy, Great Billing

Evil Lurks Beneath

Evil Death Hunter lives under the dry, solid ground.
He feeds on all types of children.
He eats them whole and spits out their clothes.
His body is big and he has a six pack.
He has pitch-black scales and red, sharp eyes.
He has red, razor-sharp fangs dripping with blood.
Never go near him!

Haylan Blomguist (8)
The Spires Academy, Great Billing

Leo The Laserbeam

Leo smells of strawberries
Me and Leo, we smell of strawberries together
Leo lives in Penny World
So do I
Our house is made out of ink
Our house is terrifying
It's the house of doom.

Jack Newton (10)
The Spires Academy, Great Billing

A Different Sunday

Lila went to the park, with her friend Mark,
on a sunny Sunday morning.
She sat on the bench with her hands in her pockets
when she suddenly heard some yawning.
She looked on the ground and all around
but then couldn't hear another sound.
What is that over there?
I think there is something under the chair.
It looks like a hare or maybe a bear.
She tiptoed towards the chair,
a smell got stronger and a sound got louder
... *thump, thump, thump!*
"Hello?" called a high-pitched voice.
"Hello?" responded Lila.
A monster anxiously came out of the bush,
(which sounded like a little whoosh!)
"Don't be scared!" Lila declared, "I'll be there for
you."
"I don't have any friends," the monster said,
"but you sound too good to be true."

Bella Hooper (10)
Walgrave Primary School, Walgrave

Goo

As I walked to school one day,
I met a monster who wanted to play,
It didn't have any name tag,
So I picked it up and put it in my bag.

It explained that its name was Goo,
He was lonely and needed a friend too.
I didn't have any friends you see,
So it bounded up and then hugged me!

I took it into school with me,
It seemed quite happy, there was lots to see!
Next, it wanted to come into class,
I had a very long test, I wanted to pass!

Luckily, the monster was very clever,
It said it wouldn't fail, never, never, never!
Goo passed the test with flying colours,
Even better, he beat loads of others!

Next, after that, it was lunch,
So my monster had a very good munch.

He got a whiff of my chip,
Jumped out of my bag and landed with a flip.

The dinner lady screamed,
And slipped on ice cream,
She banged into a kid,
Who dropped his bottle lid.

He bent down to pick it up off the floor,
Just as the head teacher walked through the door,
He took one look at all of us,
Then groaned and made a very big fuss.

"What is this mess?" he asked us crossly.
"Cleaning this up will be very costly."
We all made our way out of the hall,
Leaving a trail of slime, shiny like a glitterball!

Esther Hobbs (9)
Walgrave Primary School, Walgrave

Finally Friends

On the way home from school
I found a friend by the swimming pool.
He had green fur all over his face,
And in his hand he had a stripy suitcase.
He had two red ears protruding from the top of his head
And a broad maroon mouth for chewing up bread.
So I took him home in time for lunch
And gave him a massive food bunch!
There was bread of course
And the meat of a horse.
All on one silver plate.
He scoffed it all down so I pulled a big frown.
"This monster eats horribly," I said.
He was such a messy eater,
I didn't dare feed him chicken tikka.
I had to teach this monster a lesson,
He can't eat like this!
I grabbed a book from the shelf behind me,
It was a novel by the author Bob De Charlie.
The title read: 'Manners for Monsters'.

I couldn't believe it,
I must be bonkers!
But no, it was true,
It was the exact book I needed
So I gave it to the monster,
Hoping he could read it.
He opened the book, I watched him with glee.
He then dropped the novel, shook my hand
And we were happy as can be!
I called him Squirm Blob and we were finally friends
And this is where the story ends.

Brannon Bird (10)

Walgrave Primary School, Walgrave

Blob's Adventure

Blob lives in space, a really great place,
He came to planet Earth one day,
With his best friend named May.

He saw thousands of people who just ran away,
Then suddenly he couldn't find May.
He felt very lonely
Until there came a little boy called Tony.
"Hello," said Tony.
"Hello," Blob said.
"I'm looking for my best friend, her name is May."
"I saw her looking for you on my way."
"Really?" said Blob and off he went.
On Blob's journey he found something yummy.
"Snails," he said. He ate all three
And carried on, then he found a key.
"Where does this lead to?" Blob asked himself,
Buckingham Palace it had engraved.
Blob put it up on a shelf. "Hello," came a voice.
It was May. Blob took the key and saw a door,
The key fitted perfectly. "Are you sure?"
"Yes," said Blob.

They both stepped in
And ten corgis were barking like mad,
It scared Blob and May only a tad!

Thea Simons (9)
Walgrave Primary School, Walgrave

Fozzie

Fozzie was born in the woods,
He is Tango orange and very furry.
He is my best friend
Even though he is an ugly monster,
We are best friends forever.

We went to the museum
And had an amazing time.
Fozzie saw a dinosaur
And it made him jump,
Next we went to see Achilles
And Fozzie looked inspired.

I took him back home,
After a long day he slept under my bed.
He had a very loud snore,
It felt great having a friend,
He makes bangs and crashes,
He really is a loud monster.

The next day we had breakfast,
I showed Mum my best friend,
"Aww, he is so cute!

He is as fluffy as a bear,
We should keep him forever,
He is the cutest monster ever!"

I love Fozzie so much,
He is a great friend,
We will go out on adventures
And we will have a great life together.

Wilson Sydney Wright (9)
Walgrave Primary School, Walgrave

Tipler And Me

Creak, crack!
Is that a rat?

Scratch, scratch!
Is that my cat?

Tickle, tickle!
Is that a thistle?

Orange fur everywhere,
Leading up to my lair,
I looked under my bed,
I looked in my drawers,
Suddenly I heard a humongous roar,
My wardrobe was filled with hair and fur.
Suddenly a mouth started to talk,
Two eyes hanging on string,
Blinked at me and gave me a grin.
"Hello there, what's your name?"
"Tipler."
"Tipler," he repeated again.
He stood up tall,
His body was as big as a mule.

As he held my hand
With his lobster claws,
I put him on the sofa,
As he started to snore.
I went to bed with a yawn.

In a flash I woke up,
I'm guessing it was just a dream.

Isla Charlotte McRae (10)
Walgrave Primary School, Walgrave

The Monster Who Had Lunch With The Queen

The monster had lunch with the Queen,
She said, "You're the ugliest brute I've ever seen,
You've got a lovely mum,
But you smell of rum
And even your face is green."

The Queen was grumbling,
"Let's have tea."
The monster was so glad to sit with Her Majesty.
"You live in outer space,
Such a great place."

The monster went quiet, his mouth full,
His mouth was as big as a bull,
The Queen shouted, "Speak up boy,
Your mouth looks as fake as a plastic toy."

The monster started walking to the door,
The Queen hardly realised
As she was shocked at the dirty floor.
"Where are you going old friend?" she yelled.

But the monster didn't hear,
He was out of the door.

Isabelle Madeleine Murphy (9)
Walgrave Primary School, Walgrave

Space Monster Comes To Town

I had a dream last night,
About a monster, it gave me a fright,
His name was Crazy Creeps,
He had fuzzy hair and bright yellow teeth.

He had come from outer space,
It really was his favourite place,
I thought he was creepy,
But in the end he was friendly and slightly sneaky.

He begged me to go with him,
And in the end I gave in,
We flew to the moon and there we played,
I thought he was the best friend I had ever made.

On the way we passed the sun,
Me and him had such fun,
I never wanted to go home
And leave my best friend alone.

In the end it was time to say goodbye,
I was so sad I was about to cry,
I hope he comes back to play,
I really had a delightful day.

Olivia Sweeney (9)
Walgrave Primary School, Walgrave

The Beast With Three Heads And Twenty-Four Eyes

After school I went to a park,
I found this beast whilst it was dark.
He had three heads and twenty-four eyes,
He jumped out on me and I was surprised.

His teeth were sharp and his neck was long,
When he tried to speak it went terribly wrong.
I took him home in time for tea,
But he wouldn't even eat a pea.

I encouraged him to eat a bit,
But all he would eat was a piece of grit.
I discovered he ate boulders and rocks,
So I took him to a den dug out by a fox.
He munched at rubble, until it was gone,
Then returned to the forest, where he belonged.

I miss that beast with three heads and twenty-four eyes,
If I see him again I'll be happily surprised!

Tom Benn (10)
Walgrave Primary School, Walgrave

The Day My Monster Came To School

My monster climbed into my bag,
I didn't know until I had to present my class flag.
He made a noise,
It sounded just like my old toys.

The whole class looked at the locker
That was making the sound,
I got really nervous
Because I thought he would be found.
My teacher looked at my bag,
She glanced at the name tag,
She found out it was me
And I got detention and missed my tea.

My monster was caught,
He is still in my thoughts,
I couldn't concentrate on my work
Because my monster gave me
That special little perk.

I found him one day,
I took him back the same way,
I loved my monster so much
So I bought him a hutch.

Serena Megan Day (9)
Walgrave Primary School, Walgrave

What's Under My Bed?

What's that noise?
Maybe it's just my toys.
It's coming from under my bed,
Wait, it is glowing red.

I poke my head under
Then I hear thunder.
I jump back into bed,
Although he does look like a ted.

I hope he does not eat me,
I quite like my personality.
His teeth seem very sharp,
But I can't quite see in the dark.

I really want Mummy,
I have got butterflies in my tummy,
I want it to be morning,
When the sun is dawning.

"It's alright,
I know I am a scary sight,
I am not going to hurt you,

I am just looking for a friend."
"Well, I will be your friend."

Olivia Clarke (10)
Walgrave Primary School, Walgrave

Splodge And I!

I find a monster in my dream,
Steadily, slowly we walk along a stream,
He is ever so cute
And likes to eat fruit.

He is orange and red,
With small hairs on his head,
He has no legs, arms or feet,
And there are lots of things he likes to eat.

My monster and I,
Want to fly,
To get to space
Which is his favourite place.

We travel on his UFO,
At first it feels very low,
And then it gets so high
It feels like I am touching the sky.

I see the sun rise,
And look into his cute, cuddly eyes,

I don't want to go home,
And leave my best friend alone.

Erin Lucie Day (9)
Walgrave Primary School, Walgrave

The Monster And Me

I met a monster, big and fluffy,
I was at the park when he spotted me.
With his enormous body hanging on the swing,
He turned to face my direction,
I could not believe my eyes,
Was he a man in disguise?
I walked closer to take another look,
He seemed friendly to me,
He told me his name was Mr Chubby,
Should I tell him mine?
Should I see if he wants a friend?
We played on the swing, we played on the slide,
We even played on the see-saw,
He made me smile, after all he was a friendly monster,
From now on it is just me and the monster.

Chanel Fury (10)
Walgrave Primary School, Walgrave

Firelord

When I went to school I bumped into a monster,
His name was Firelord.
At school he was not called in the register
So he said, "You didn't call me!"
"Okay Firelord, yes!"
Firelord ate nothing and played a lot,
He liked to fly
But he wasn't allowed to go outside the school.
He was very kind and very helpful,
Nothing made him sad,
He spoke our language.
He was eight years old.
Everyone liked him.
One day he wasn't at school
And everyone got sad
And then he came back
And everybody had a party.

Oliver Jeffery (9) & Harrison Singh Hammond

Walgrave Primary School, Walgrave

The Monster In The Dishwasher

The monster in the dishwasher,
As red as a furious fire.
The monster in the dishwasher,
Beware he has hideous horns.
The monster from the dishwasher,
He has no friends.
The monster in the dishwasher,
Slimy and gory, making the dishes dirty.
The monster in the dishwasher,
Breaking all the cutlery.
The monster from the dishwasher,
Trying not to make a sound,
Only hoping to make a lifelong friend,
Hoping for someone to notice his kindness.
The monster in the dishwasher,
As kind as can be,
With his new friend, Mr T.

Iris Jones (9)
Walgrave Primary School, Walgrave

The Trickster

The trickster travelled to a wood on her broom,
This dangerous beast so small but feisty,
Slumped down on a bench
Holding a lead attached to a dog called Zog.

A little girl came up to the monstrous predator,
She had a sympathetic smile,
They soon became friends,
The girl thought it would never end.

The devious devil took the being to the park,
That is where they had a few laughs,
The stench of Nobbles seemed to come closer.
Soon after the fierce breath dropped down your neck.

Yum, yum, she's in my tum!

Shana Simone Odell (10)

Walgrave Primary School, Walgrave

Rapid Fire

I went to the bank and saw a monster at the till.
Then a robber came and stuck a gun at me.
Then I ran really far.
Then the monster whacked him with a broken jar.
After that he swung away.
Everyone shouted, "Hip hip hooray!"

He had three horns and had four legs,
He also had no friends.
His body was orange and his teeth were blue.
Maybe someday he'll meet you.

He flew back to the sun.
He had to run from a police gun.
Although he stopped the evil man
The police still had to take him down.

Theo Collins (9)
Walgrave Primary School, Walgrave

My Friend Called Meck

I saw a monster,
Which was eating a lobster,
I went over there
To see if it had hair.
We played with a kite,
Then pretended to be knights,
He hated to sleep,
As daytime was his treat.
We woke up in a mess,
So we had to get dressed.
We went over to a palm tree,
To see the sea.
We went on the beach,
And what we saw was a tasty little treat.
We went over to eat,
It turned into a feast.
It was time to say goodbye
Which almost made me cry.
Was it a dream
Or was it something I'd seen?

Ed Bond (10)
Walgrave Primary School, Walgrave

There's A Beast In My Bedroom

One night my eyes were shut tight,
It was the middle of the night,
I woke up and a monster flew through the window,
I didn't know what was happening.

I was scared at first
But when we played
I wasn't scared anymore,
Look at the mess we had made.

She was as bright as a balloon
With a shimmering smile
That glowed all night long.

When we were tired we cuddled up in bed
And fell fast asleep,
When I woke up in the morning
My monster was gone,
Was it just a dream?

Freya Elizabeth Perkins (10)
Walgrave Primary School, Walgrave

The Monster Ham Ham Saves The Day

In the woods, flying high, ham monsters delve in the sky.

One ham monster, so peaceful, its name is Ham Ham.

Ham Ham was so fluffy he was like a bunny.

He always liked his freedom, but if us humans needed him he'd be there.

One day, he was flying high but then he heard a cry.

It was for help, so he was there as quick as lightning.

The train was coming off the track, he saved the day and he felt so happy.

He decided to live happily with humans till the day's end.

The end, till he saves the day again!

Poppie Davidson Murphy (9)
Walgrave Primary School, Walgrave

My Monster And Me

He's good, not bad,
He is very rarely sad,
He's orange and white,
He comes out at night.

I saw him in the dark
Next to his spaceship called The Spark.
The driver was called Mark,
It was black and white
With a tint of delight.
He came in through the door
And his jokes were very poor.
There were smiles and tears,
They were listening with all ears.
His eyes were blue with a tint of black
As dark as a cupboard with the door shut.

Isaac Ellis (9)
Walgrave Primary School, Walgrave

Mr Slimy

Mr Slimy lives in Ireland,
He has one hair, the rest is bare.
He has one leg, the other is a peg.
He is extremely disgusting.
He's got lots of talent
Such as dancing and prancing
And showing off his peg leg.

He won Monster Got Talent
Which allowed him to perform for the Queen.
He span on his head and jumped on her bed.
The guards said, "Off with his head!"
So he ran down the stairs,
Stomp, stomp, stomp!
Off he went!

Tommy Hooper (9)
Walgrave Primary School, Walgrave

Monster Day

I met a monster, massive and fluffy,
We went to the park,
He turned his face towards me,
He walked to me.

"I am from Mars,
Can I be your friend?"
"Yes."
"My name is Monster Day."
He was a very protective friend.

The monster followed me to my house,
He was a good monster.

We went back to the park.
We played on the swings.
We played on the slide.
I was happy that I'd got a new friend.

Joshua Sweet (10)
Walgrave Primary School, Walgrave

L-Drago

There once was a dragon called L-Drago,
Its eyes gleam with a piercing bright yellow,
It eats magma, drinks lava,
Burns crops, hates water drops.

Has no pains, always sees flames,
Hears fire, creates smoke,
Hates humans, makes them choke,
Tastes ash, feels heat,
Breathes fire at living meat.

L-Drago is a legend,
It wants to cause an Armageddon,
If you ever destroy L-Drago,
Your eyes will turn a very bright yellow!

Fraser MacPhail (10)
Walgrave Primary School, Walgrave

Royal Sleepover

I once met a guy called Flopsy High
Who was a fly on the Queen's thigh.
He flew over some cities,
Seeing the world's big life.

Through the night soaring in the sky,
While I sat upon his silky ear
His excitement was high,
His mouth full of pie.
When we arrived at Buckingham Palace
I saw all his friends and the royals.

We all slept over and watched movies,
Then went to school
The next day together.

Jessica-Louise Jeffery (10)
Walgrave Primary School, Walgrave

On My Way To School

This morning on my way to school
I bumped into a monster as you do.
He was around five foot two,
He had spikes on his back
And a big round mouth.
He had claws on his hands
And they were very sharp indeed,
He was very hard to feed.

When we got to school
My teacher called the register,
The monster came out of nowhere,
He was acting cool and funny,
He really was too cool for school!

William Wren (9)
Walgrave Primary School, Walgrave

The Bobby

On the way to the park,
My monster explored,
He found a chocolate bar
And a big roar.

Around the corner we went,
Up and down near the tent,
Bobby ran and ran,
Until he found a fan.

He's from the sun,
And we all know he's dumb,
He is scary,
He is also very hairy.

He eats meat,
And has smelly feet,
He is flying,
Oh no, he's dying.

Charles William Howard Burditt (10)

Walgrave Primary School, Walgrave

Miss Hart

I once met a princess
Her name was Miss Hart
She liked making people happy
Especially her papey.

Princess Hart went to Papey's
On the way she got hungry
When she got there she made tarts
Then she played the harp.

Getting ready
Putting on her hat
Going home
Flying her drone.

Getting home
Finishing her poem
Going to bed
Banging her head.

Charlotte Murphy (10)
Walgrave Primary School, Walgrave

My Monster

The evil beast
Came from the east,
It ran and ran
From the mean man.

Its friends have gone
On the streets no light shone,
It came for me,
It sat on my knee.

Like an animal
As fast as a cannonball
His eyes are red, he's close to dead,
He made a bang.

Nowhere to be seen,
My monster is gone,
Now light has shone.

Taylor Linnell (10)
Walgrave Primary School, Walgrave

Friends

I met a monster, cute and fluffy,
We went to the park,
He turned towards me,
He ran to me.

"I am from Heaven,
Can I be your friend?"
"Yes you can."
He is a very protective monster.

The monster followed me to school,
He is a happy monster,
We went to the park
And played on the swings!

Darcie Quigley (9)
Walgrave Primary School, Walgrave

Rusty's Life

My friend is a monster,
He's super slimy,
His name is Rusty.
He lives in a granary in Dusty.
He went to a school in Dusty
But he left the school
Because he was too much of a slow coach
And that's why he left the school.
Rusty passed the ball,
A boy called Raul came.
Raul and Rusty became friends.

Kye Hansen (9)
Walgrave Primary School, Walgrave

Bob's Day At School

Bob is a monster,
He's cute, fluffy and tall.
He's friendly and he follows me to school.
He makes me jump
Every time he walks through the door.
He says hello to my friends
But all he does is roar!
At lunch he eats slime.

Rachel Leonard (9)
Walgrave Primary School, Walgrave

Monster Takes Over The Universe

A monster that's ugly and slimy
Walks the Earth to threaten the universe.

His teeth are as hard as a knife.
His nose is as gooey as a mud bath.
His eyes are monster eyes.
His hair is like a dog's tail.

Oscar Newberry (9)
Walgrave Primary School, Walgrave

YOUNG WRITERS INFORMATION

We hope you have enjoyed reading this book – and that you will continue to in the coming years.

If you're a young writer who enjoys reading and creative writing, or the parent of an enthusiastic poet or story writer, do visit our website **www.youngwriters.co.uk**. Here you will find free competitions, workshops and games, as well as recommended reads, a poetry glossary and our blog.

If you would like to order further copies of this book, or any of our other titles, then please give us a call or visit **www.youngwriters.co.uk**.

Young Writers
Remus House
Coltsfoot Drive
Peterborough
PE2 9BF
(01733) 890066
info@youngwriters.co.uk